Single Parenting

Ways to Prevent the Ultimate Breakage

Patrice Met

Dedication

For everyone out there who has taken the pains of single parenting!

I dedicate this book to you!

Acknowledgment

I would like to thank everyone who turned this book into a reality. From my editors and advisors to my friends and family, this book is a product of the courage you gave me to move forward with my ideas and author my own book!

Preface

This book is both a warning and a guide for those who have an ear for it. If you have not yet become a single parent, you can use this book to avoid becoming one! If fate has already made up its mind about your destiny than you can use this book to learn ways of becoming an exceptional single parent! Learn several ways to prevent the ultimate breakage.

Contents

Introduction

"I don't think I realized how stressed I was, being a single parent. It was really, really stressful. It's not easy on anybody."

-Reese Witherspoon

This quote from the famous actress Reese Witherspoon puts in perspective that no one is immune to becoming a single parent. It has almost become a trend nowadays that people are becoming single parents. It is hard for each and everyone no matter how much help you have, it will always make you question your efforts. You must find the motivation that you are one of the many people who is raising children all alone and if they can do it so can you.

What does this Book Offer?

The premise of this book is to help you avoid making mistakes which might affect your personal life in the worst possible ways. This book will discuss with you ways with which you can avoid becoming a single parent. It will elaborate on the things you need to be careful about, things you are supposed to do and not supposed to do. Through this book, you will also learn how to judge whether or not you are heading down a path of becoming a single parent. To become a single parent, you don't need to be married or anything. A lot of people end up becoming single parents without being married and in their teenage years. This book will guide you about how to avoid becoming a single parent in the first place. In addition, it will show you ways to prevent breakage from your children if you do end up single parenting eventually.

Furthermore, this book will discuss how you can cope with becoming a single parent if you have found yourself stuck in this situation. This book contains discussions on how you can raise your kids skillfully as a single parent whether you are a mother or father. This book will be able to identify authentic institutions who can assist you in your tireless efforts.

You can get financial, emotional or social help with raising your kids properly. This book will especially help you if you are living in the United States of America, Canada or Australia.

As we move forward in this book, you will learn several strategies to tell your children exactly what happened with you and your partner and how you ended up a single parent. This process is vital because parents generally struggle with this and this ends up hurting them and the kids just as much. This will book take you through step by step ways to help you in staying successful in your single parenting.

Lastly, in this book, you will get to learn how you can maintain a healthy relationship with your children after they reach their teenage years because those are the hardest on you and your child. When you have a meaningful relationship and a strong bond with your kids, you can avoid breakage with them, which is the toughest scenario for all the single parents and kids out there!

Let's take this journey together to establish a way of living which will benefit both you and your future generations.

Chapter 1
How to Avoid becoming a Single Parent?

Teen Pregnancy

Single parenting is the result of an incident in your life that may have been pleasant or unpleasant at the time. Its reasons may include divorce, break-up, and abandonment, death of the other parent, teenage pregnancy, single-person adoption or artificial insemination. All these incidents are unpleasant except for single-person adoption and artificial insemination. No one wants such events to happen in their lives. The exceptions have something good to offer in the lives of individuals who hope for them.

Other instances are highly unwelcomed, and they need to be prevented for living a good life. It is really hard being a single parent since you become responsible for taking care of your children with finances as well as supporting them emotionally and physically. There are many challenges in being a single parent. There is always a discussion about the challenges that new parents face, but when you take the (s) out of the parents and put single behind it, the challenges for a single parent become tenfold. Taking the partner in crime element out of the equation makes it really difficult to bring balance in your life. A lot of single parents struggle with the same emotions. They have anxiety over money and have self-doubt over the decisions they are making. When you become a single parent, you have everything coming your way at the same time, and you're dealing with it all alone.

You end up feeling tension, stress, and anxiety. As a single parent, you have to face the fact that you are going to be raising your kids without support from your life partner. Taking care of your children as a single parent is stressful. Sometimes, you feel stressed out because you have to take care of yourself along with your kids.

For example, you have to do daily chores, your job, and other routines which require your attention as well. No one wants to raise children on their own, and many don't intend on becoming single parents. When such a situation ends up happening to you, then you have to deal with it in a way that it doesn't affect you or your children in a way that hurts you beyond repair.

In 2017, 194,337 babies were born to women aged between 15-19 years in the U.S. Although this may be a record low for the U.S. teen pregnancy rate which dropped 7% from 2016, there is still a possibility of teen pregnancy. The rate of teen pregnancy in the U.S is still quite higher than that of other western countries

Let me first discuss why prevention is essential.

Importance of Preventing Teen Pregnancies

Teen pregnancy and childbearing not only adds to the social cost but also adds to the economic cost. It affects the teen parents and their children immediately and all through the years to come. In many cases, the teen withdraws from school, and their social life is completely devastated because they feel rejection and face derogatory comments and statements.

Friendships break since many parents of other children see the teen parent as an unfit role model for their children. You cannot blame them for wanting the best for their children. Mistakes must be avoided so that teen pregnancy can be eradicated. There are a lot of things to look at on many spectrums. Preventing teen pregnancy is an effort that has to be a joint effort by parents, teachers, and teens evenly. Everyone needs to play their part in order to prevent teen pregnancies truly.

Some figures show just how much impact teen pregnancy has on the economy and some general statements taken from studies and from professors over this subject.

- Pregnancy and birth are the most significant contributors to high school dropout rates among girls. Only 50% of the teen mothers receive a high school diploma by the age of 22. While almost 90% of women who do not give birth in their adolescence to graduation from high school.

- The children of mothers who were pregnant as a teenager are more likely to have lower school achievements and are more like to drop out of high school. They are more likely to have health problems because teenage mothers don't have much clue about what they are doing. Since they themselves are children, they can hardly take care of themselves let alone another small very delicate human being. Children of teenage mothers are more likely to be incarcerated at some time during their adolescence as well because of lack of proper guidance. They are also more likely to suffer the same fate that their teenage mother suffered. All of this could be because of negligence from the mother because the mother herself is a kid and has little to no idea about what is required to raise a child properly, in a way that will benefit her children. In her days of playing and worrying about her SATs, she is worried about what will happen to her child.

Realizing that there is a problem, is the first step to solving any problems that may arise with this teen pregnancy. Understanding the consequences that the teenage parent or the newborn children could face is important in this case. There are a lot of ways one can prevent their kid from having this fate. The parents of the single parent, their school and the teens themselves have to stay focused.

Let's look at the roles that should be played by parents and then we will come to the roles that should be played by schools and then teens themselves.

Roles of Parents in Preventing Teen Pregnancies

For parents, when it comes to their teenage children, most of the times the word sex is a big NO. Often times, parents live in a bubble. While in this bubble, they believe that their kids are not as mischievous as they had been in their childhood. Every parent believes that their child is more or less a saint who would never indulge in any sexual activity. However, this belief shakes pretty severely when their one or more of their teens end up becoming a single parent.

By creating this picture-perfect image of their kids, parents put their teens on a pedestal. As a result, they end up not only hurting themselves but their children as well. Because they believe that their children couldn't possibly do something of this sort, they fail to realize that sexual development is a normal part for their teens' lives.

Teenagers need their parents' help in understanding their feelings, helping them in dealing with peer pressure and how to say no if they don't want to have sex. If and when your teen becomes sexually active you need to tell them the ways they can use to prevent pregnancy and stay safe from catching sexually transmitted diseases. Teens want to talk to their parents about sex and relationships, but when they see that their parents might disapprove of them because of that, they end up concealing the truth from them. They also don't seek advice from their friends which again harms them. Parents should stay prepared that their children are going to grow up one day and they will have sexual desires that would need containing.

They should have an attitude which allows them to help their children in keeping them from making any unwanted mistakes. They will need to advise their children in a timely manner. Parents have a substantial impact on whether their teenager makes a healthy decision or makes an unhealthy one. The same goes for sex as well.

Parents can tell them when to start having sex and that it is okay if they stay don't indulge in any sexual activity during their high school years. Parents have to tell them that it's okay not to have sex and that it is okay to say no. Parents must be able to tell their teenagers what peer pressure can do, and they must warn them of the consequences they could face if they make bad choices.

Don't discourage them and tell them all of this in a way where they might feel as if they are being attacked. Remember, teenagers are very sensitive, and they are just finding themselves. They are full of pride and if they will sense even a little bit of offense, they can get defensive and won't ever come to you regarding anything let alone sex.

For parents, there are a lot of things that you can do to help your children open up to you. It is going to sound harsh and daunting in the beginning, but as parents get into this habit, they will find that it will get easier eventually.

Establish clear values towards sex:

- Firstly, parents need to establish their own values and attitudes towards sex. They need to be clear on a few things before they can start talking to their children. Parents need to ask themselves these questions before they can start asking their teenager their own set of questions.

    > How I feel about high school teenagers being sexually active?

> Who should be setting the sexual limits in a relationship and how will this limit be set?
> Was I sexually active as a high schooler? How do I feel about it all now? Was I sexually active before I got married to my wife? How will the answer to these questions affect my child?
> What do I think about teenagers using contraceptives like condoms and birth control pills?

Parents should ask themselves these question before they say anything to their children because these are all the questions a teenager will generally ask you when you sit them down to talk about sex. If you don't have it clear in your head how you feel about the subject then surely they won't be clear about it either.

Talk about sex with your kids

- Parents must talk to their children about sex and love early on in their teenage. They should bring up this subject often. Parents need to try being specific when they are talking about sex and love. The most important thing in this whole conversation would be the first part of it. Parents need to be honest with their child and also have to be open about it; vague answers and responses won't do. Remember teenagers are growing up in an age where information is readily available. If they catch their parents telling half-truths, it might break the entire trust system and teenagers being hormonally charged human beings that they are, might stop talking to their parents completely if they don't trust them. Parents need to understand that talking about sex won't necessarily mean that this encourages your teenagers to have sex. What this will do in turn will be that they will begin to understand what sex is and when it is right to have it.

Parents need to set down the difference between love and infatuation first, especially for girls. Liking a boy is fine but giving up her virginity to that boy is wrong. Parents need to sit their little girl down and tell her that they support her, but she needs to focus on herself as well. Parents need to tell their children about how relationships work and how healthy relationship functions. Parents must tell their children the difference between love and sex and tell their children about the values and beliefs they hold themselves. After the discussions and conversations, parents need to play sound role models for their children as well. They have to walk the talk. It is important for children to be able to ask their parents questions about sex. Parents must try their best to be approachable. They need to let their kids know that they can talk to them about anything and everything. After saying this, parents must be patient and answer their kids politely and in the best way for them to understand even if the parents think the question is something disrespectful.

What are the questions that kids could ask you about sex and love?

- How do I know I'm in love? Won't sex bring me closer to my significant other?
- How will I know when I am ready for marriage? How will I know I am ready for sex?
- Will having sex make me more popular in school? Will I become more mature and act more grown up after having sex?
- How do contraceptives work? Which one is the best? Which one is the safest?

- How do I tell my significant other I don't want to have sex?

- How do I respond to pressure from my significant other?

- Is getting pregnant easy? What is required to get pregnant?

Parents can similarly respond to their kids with these answers

- I think kids in high school are too young to have sex and understand it completely. There is more to it than just a physical bond.

- Whenever you have sex, you need to make sure you always use protection to prevent pregnancy and STDs unless you are trying to conceive a child.

- Teens today find themselves in many sexually charged situations. Think ahead about how you will handle this? Will, you straight up say no or will you use contraception? You should think things through before making up your mind.

- It is perfectly natural and okay to have sexual desires, because if you don't have it in your teens then when do you get them? What's not okay is for teens to get pregnant.

- Having sex won't make you more mature or more popular; it could actually hurt your reputation in a negative way.
- Having sex shouldn't be something that is required to get close to your significant other.
- If your boyfriend/girlfriend is pressurizing you into having sex than they aren't right for you and are not with you for you.

Supervise and monitor your kids

After becoming a friend to their children, parents must get back to their duties of parenting and start by supervising and monitoring their children's activities. You have to know where your children are at all times. Are they protected? What are they doing? Are they involved in useful activities or not? If they aren't with you, are they being supervised by responsible adults?

Know their friends and their families

Parents must start by knowing their children's friends and their families. Teenagers are highly influenced by their surroundings and especially their friends. So parents have to make sure that their children are hanging around positive influence. Parents must make sure that their kids are friends with other children who come from a family with similar values as their own. Parents must welcome their children's friends in their house and talk to them normally as they would talk to their own children. This will give their friends a sense of love, and they will become more likely to respect the values set down by you as a parent. Parents can further talk to their kid's friend's parents as well to set down curfew and common rules and expectations.

Clear your views about dating someone older than your kids

Make sure you are clear to your teenager about your views on them dating someone who is far older or far younger than they are. Try setting a limit of no more than 2 years of age difference both ways. A significant age gap can lead to risky situations and unprotected sex.

Help your kids set future goals:

Help your kids in setting future goals for themselves and motivate them towards a career path of their liking. If your child likes to dance, encourage them to take part in musicals and tell them how their options will look in the future and give them ambitions about their life, something that will be more attractive to them than early pregnancy and parenthood.

Make education their priority

Emphasize on education. Set high but real expectations from your children's school performance. If your child is not performing well in school, you should intervene in the start and try and help them get better. Keep track of your child's school work and meet with teachers. Keep your children busy by encouraging them to take on extra-curricular activities such as joining the editorial board or debates teams. This will keep them busy and give them a sense of achievement as well, which won't just give them confidence boost but will also prevent them to look for ways that fulfill the need of being popular that almost every teen has.

Know what your kids are being exposed to in the name of entertainment:

Keep an eye on what your kids are watching, reading or listening to. In a world where everything is readily available, and everything is in front of your children. With them having phones and computers they are able to access almost anything they wish to see. You apparently cannot take their phones away from them and take parental control to an extreme level.

But what you can do is that you can help your children think critically and talk with them about what they are learning from the programs they are watching and the music they are listening to. Ask them to share what they like to watch and listen to with you. This won't only portray you as cool but will also allow you to keep an eye on them discreetly Parents need to be especially vigilant about their children since they can be influenced by them. But that doesn't mean that parents are the only people that can prevent teens from unprotected sex and getting pregnant. As mentioned above, schools play a huge role in all of this as well.

Role of Schools in Preventing Teen Pregnancies

On average children start going to school at the age of 5 and they stay in school up until their early 20s if you add college into the mix. Public schools serve 50 million children in the United States alone, so the responsibility of schools and teachers are immense. Children spend 8-9 hours each day in school. This is where they get most of their influence from.

Schools need to understand that what they are doing right now it is just not working. There are a lot of things they can do to make everything better; from bullying to teen pregnancy.

Sex education crisis:

- First things first let's address how schools treat sex education. A lot of times there is a speaker that comes in the class and shows a pregnancy video and then tells the entire class not to have sex. Some children don't even get sex education and learn everything from the internet which is one of the main reasons teen pregnancy went to such a high rate in the 90s.

Why is it so hard for teens to get quality sexual education? Firstly sex education is not mandatory in most of the states in the US and those that do teach sex education very few of them teach it in a methodical way that benefits the students. The first rule of business for schools must be that they should have comprehensive sex education and this is what it looks like. A lot of times sex education in a lot of institutions all around the United States is not medically accurate. Sex education is held at a completely different level than classes like English, history or math.

Which is astonishing since far more people need to know how to prevent pregnancy in their adulthood than how to find an angle on an isosceles triangle. Sex education should have the same approach as education for drivers. People understand fully how important it is to teach teenagers how to drive safely. It is no difference when it comes to having sex. Having unprotected sex doesn't only increase the chances of getting pregnant but also involves chances of different kinds of STDs. Lessons about safe sex should be normalized

Emphasis on education:

Just like parents should encourage their child to have an excellent academic standing and get grades that will help them follow their ambitions to the utmost of their ability. Similarly, schools should promote academic success. Not only will it improve the teenager's confidence but it will also increase their self-worth and allow them to see a bigger picture than the bubble most teenagers live in.

Counseling for success:

Schools can further everything by having a good life counselor who could be put mandatory for students to see. Life counselor won't only help teenagers in realizing their ambitions and that there is more to life than just high school. It will also take them out of the element of thinking that sex is the only way they can gain popularity. This will also give them a sense of direction which will motivate them even more towards their goal.

Have a wide range of extra-curricular activities:

Schools can have more extra-curricular activities available. Schools generally only have few extra-curricular activities to offer. It's either sports in which only a handful of people could partake in. And the other activities which are present are either debates or theatre. There is nothing wrong with these activities but these won't jive with everyone. Having a wide variety of extra-curricular activities, like a chess club, rotary club, editorial boards, eSport club, music society and so forth. This will allow teens to pursue things that interest them and will enable them to meet people with similar interest. Not only will it increase fulfillment in their lives but will also have a benefit in their social life as well.

Schools try their best to play a part in protecting children from pregnancy and STDs but what has been done recently isn't working. Politicians and administration should understand that they are living in the 21st century and the methods and sexual educations that worked 3 decades ago aren't working anymore. So they should open their minds and change the perspective they hold of sex educations promoting more sex.

It's not only the responsibility of schools and parents to prevent teenage pregnancy, but it is also the responsibility of the party directly involved in the situation. Boys and girls who indulge in sexual activities must understand the consequences of their actions.

Teens should understand that sex is not the only thing in a relationship and getting intimate is more than just knowing each other physically.

Roles of Teens in Preventing Teen Pregnancies

First things first, teens need to understand that their lives have just started and there will be a lot of time for sex, love and everything else that they think that is so important right now. Teenagers must realize the importance of school and the urgency of their ambitions. They must get serious with themselves and truly understand that these are the years that they have right now and will be gone in a blink of an eye.

Decide not to have sex:

- What teens can do in the first place is that they can opt out of having sex at the beginning of their teen years where they don't know much about anything. That is the safest bet at that time. When teens are feeling such strong hormonal changes, they don't know how to share anything and find talking to their parents hard and awkward.

Talk to elders about sex:

- Teens can act responsible and talk to their elders. Whether a teacher or a parent, they must learn where to get birth control and other contraceptives if they choose to be sexually active.

Seek out information:

- If proper education is not provided, that doesn't mean that this gives a teenager a free rein. A teenager must act responsibly and must seek out knowledge about prevention so that they can better equip themselves for anything in the future. Asking the internet is not recommended, teens must contact a health care provider or talk to their parents directly.

These are some of the tools to bring the rate of teenage pregnancy even lower. It is true that the rate of teenage pregnancy has seen a significant drop in these past years as mentioned above. But still, a much lower rate is required to say that we have done something significant.

How to Prevent being Divorced/Broken Up

Teenage pregnancy isn't the only way people end up as single parents, but there can be a lot of other reasons as well. People are married, and their spouse dies, or they get divorced or their significant other breaks up with them. All of these can be reasons people end up a single parent. But you can't do much about these reasons as you can for teenage pregnancy.

But there is still hope, and there are still a few ways you can strengthen your relationship with your spouse or significant other.

- Firstly you need to be willing to prevent divorce. You need to be able to put the pouting and anger aside and get ready to work hard. Actions speak louder than words. This is truer when trying to prevent divorce. If you and your spouse are ready to prevent divorce, then both of you have to stop playing the blame game, quit the excuses and the fighting and get ready to put everything in front of each other.

- You must be willing to hold yourself accountable. When you and your partner are speculating divorce, keep in mind that if you start with accusatory questions that will only make matters worse. You must be the one to stop pointing the finger and approach your spouse or significant other with a sense of self-accountability. By doing so, both you and your partner will be able to see each other's side of the story and will come up with a solution other than divorce.

- Communicate effectively. There is nothing worse than speaking to your spouse in a condescending manner in a marriage that is already on the rocks. Keeping your tone and language productive will help you to strengthen the bond once again with your partner.

- Clear out all the grudges you have with your partner and be serious about making it work. Holding grudges will only lead to future fights, airing out your issues and taking a serious step to forgiving will enable you both to move forward.

Now let us focus on what needs to be done once people end up as single parents. Because let's face it there is nothing no one can do to stop this from happening in the end. So what should a single parent do when they find themselves with a kid and standing there all alone?

SINGLE PARENTING

Chapter 2
How to be a Successful Single Parent?

Single parents have become more common than ever. There are a lot of problems that a single parent has to deal with — ranging from their kids getting sick or doing poorly in school to their own mental health and financial problems. They have to face all of these problems alone. The good part is that there is a lot of help available to single parents and people have become more open to single parenthood more than ever.

Following are some tips that might help any single parent reading this book:

Have a good support system

- A single parent can often feel isolated and overwhelmed because of all the responsibilities they have on their hands. So that's why it is so important to have a support team behind you. When a single parent starts taking care of their baby, they might get overrun by emotions and might feel as thou they have too much on their plate. They think to themselves that they have no one else to help them with all this. By a support team, I mean that you should always have some people that have your back around you. These people could include your parents, your siblings and y our best friend. Single parents must realize that there is no shame for asking help and it is almost impossible for them to raise their kids properly when done alone. Although there are people who do accomplish this but those people feel burned out and overwhelmed more often than people that ask for help from those they love

Avoid taking on more than you can handle

- Avoid following into the supermom and super dad trap. Single parents must understand that they cannot work all day come home and get the house super clean, cook up a nice hot dinner and tend to their children's needs. Single parents need to be realistic and understand what they can and cannot accomplish in a day. Single parents should feel the need to overcompensate if they are going through a divorce or are a single parent by any other means. Serving cereal for breakfast and have fast food meals for some dinners is entirely okay, as long as your child's overall diet is healthy. It's okay to have a less-than-spotless house if that means you will be able to give more time to your kids.

Say goodbye to guilt

- A Single parent has to say goodbye to guilt. No matter what the reason one has of becoming a single parent. There is a nagging voice that almost every single parent has inside of them that hurts them continuously. It might say things about them working too much or too little, have less time or for their kids. Having fights with their ex, thinking that the life your kids lead is because of them and they are to blame for everything wrong. Or the general feeling that the family is not complete and is broken in a sense that it might hurt their child in the long run.

While it is always easy to find a thing to blame themselves about and feel guilty about it, it's better to focus on what's good and right about their family rather than on the things that are lacking and are wrong. Asking themselves whether their kids are being given every necessity, are their wants and wishes being fulfilled, and is your house a warm and happy place to be at. Looking at the brighter side of things won't only have a high impact on you but by seeing you in a jolly and happy going mood your kids will be affected in a positive way as well.

Make time for yourself

- As a single parent, it is essential to have some time on your own as well. It is vital to schedule downtime in your life to rest and refuel. These 'time-offs' don't need to be every day. You can start off by marking off just two dates over the next four weeks. These days are just for you. You can hire a babysitter or swap child-care duties with a friend and go out and do what you enjoy. Go shopping, go to a yoga class or go see a movie. Additionally give yourself one night a week to set aside chores, work, and any other obligation and do something for yourself after your kids have gone to bed: read a book, catching up with a friend or taking a nice relaxing hot bubble bath. Building these small 'me time' into your life will help maintain your stamina that you require in raising your kids.

Spend time with your kids

- One of the key things in staying motivated and happy as a single parent is to spend time with your kids. After all, all the hard work you do and the perseverance you have is because of them. So spending time with your children will satisfy your deep need for meaningful interaction and purpose. Seeing them happy, smiling and laughing, you could then say to yourself that all that hard is paying off by itself. So whenever you come back home after a tiring day, you could set aside some time to spend with your kids. You can always put aside some of the obligations you think you have and indulge in some quality time with your kids. This will instantly sift your true priorities from those things that are non-essential.

Stay positive

- Maintaining a positive attitude is one of the utmost responsibility one has as a single parent. It is very easy to feel sad and hunch your shoulders and accept defeat. Remember your attitude is entirely contagious. Not only will it affect your kids' ability to handle everyday ups and downs, but it will also have the power to impact whether the future for your family is born of hope or despair. One of the ways you can battle these feelings of negativity is by keeping a journal. Writing things down will only make it easier on the nerves and body. Keeping a journal and writing down the challenges you face every day will also lead you in solving them after seeing them written down in front of you. It will become easier to go through your problems and coming up with a solution.

Set down rules and regulations

- Setting down house rules and regulation is another key aspect of being a successful single parent. Explain the house rules and the expectations you have of your child, such as speaking respectfully, having dinner at a particular time and going to sleep at a certain time. Enforcing them in a way that the child doesn't feel attacked is key. Work with other caregivers in your child's life to provide consistent discipline. You must be careful not to seem too strict, consider re-evaluating some limits such as screen times and bedtimes as your child grows older. This will result in them respecting your limits and will give them the ability to accept more responsibility.

Find good child care:

- Finding quality child care is one of the, if not the most important thing a single parent has to do. You might need regular childcare. You need to look for experienced caregivers who can provide stimulation in a safe and healthy environment. Someone who your child will be comfortable with. Don't rely on older children from your block to babysit only. There are special services that provide experience and qualified caregivers. You can always ask an old friend to look after your kids, but always be careful asking a new friend or someone who you have been dating to look after your kids. Only because you cannot trust just anyone around your kids and your kids need to be comfortable around them as well.

Love your children

- Lastly, remember to show your love to your children. With you working almost all day your child will long for your attention. Make sure to give them proper praise and kiss them on the cheeks and tell them you love them. Give them unconditional love and try and not let the stress of work and other responsibilities be a hurdle in you loving your child.

Don't talk down your ex-partner:

- Lastly make sure to not talk about down to your ex-partner, or your kids mom or dad. When you get a divorce, it is easy to start badmouthing and thinking about the mistakes your partner made or how they are the reason you are in this situation. There are psychological impacts of badmouthing the other parent on your child. First and foremost, it's hurtful to your child. No matter what parents do, it's natural for most children to continue to love their parents unconditionally and seek their acceptance and approval. When anyone puts down someone or something we love, it hurts, and it hurts all the more if the person doing the putting down is your other parent. In addition to them feeling hurt, it can put them in a position where they may feel like they have to choose a side. Children love both of their parents unconditionally, and when they would feel that they are being influenced to love one or the other more, they are going to experience a tremendous amount of guilt and shame. Due to the lack of tools they have for expressing themselves, all of this turns inwards. Children contain it, and it can lead to poor self-esteem, self-blaming, and self-hatred which can lead to substance abuse, legal problems, eating disorders and self-injurious behaviors. The best thing you can do for your child is to try to get along with your ex in a civil way. Try to remember why you fell in love with your partner in the first place, and share the positive aspects of the other parent with your child. In any case, if you can't say anything nice, don't say anything at all.

As a single parent, you are going to feel lonely, and you are going to think that you too require a partner to share your worries and happy times with. It is inevitable a single parent has to get back out there, and they have to start dating again. Single parenting and taking care of children all on your own is hard enough as it is, throwing in dating to that tornado is going to make it even harder. It will be hard, and it might get messy, but you have to do it, not just for your own sake but for your little one's sake as well.

Chapter 3
How to Date as a Single Parent?

There are a lot of ways you can be a success in the dating world as a single parent. Here are a few tips and strategies you can use so that you can have a good dating life.

Don't start dating immediately after breaking up from your first relationship:

- First things first, as a single parent give yourself some time, it is advised that you should wait at least a year before starting off and dating. Single parents who start dating too quickly after they become a single parent whether by any means make their children more resilient to your partner. This sabotages the ability of a step-parent and the step-child to get off on the right foot with one another and puts the family at risk.

Date to start a family, not a relationship

- A single parent must realize that they are not a teen anymore and dating would mean that you are creating a family, not a relationship. It is especially hard for your children to understand this because here is where the competing elements start. You with your partner will create insecurities with your children. The choice of being with the dating partner or the children is generally the feeling of left on the waiting list. This might hurt your children and make them think how their relationship with you is being affected by the other person. Wise single parents realize this and assume that becoming a couple won't necessarily mean that you are going to bring the other person in your family right away. So they tend to both and take time assessing how the potential stepfamily relationship is going to develop.

Be open about being a single parent

- Being open about the fact that you are a single parent. This is the thing a lot of people have trouble in. If you have an online dating profile, then mention that you are a single parent, if you meet someone and they ask you out, or you ask someone out make sure to tell them your situation. Because you want to avoid attracted someone who is not right and okay with your life.

Be proud of your life:

- Be proud, never excuse, apologize or defend yourself. You don't need to explain yourself to your partner in the beginning. How you became, a single parent is none of anyone's business but yours. Be proud of your family and your life. Know that anyone who will enter your life will be lucky to get such a fantastic family.

Have a positive attitude towards dating:

- Feel positive about wanting to date. Never think that you are doing something when thinking about wanting some time for yourself. You might feel a pang of guilt when you get all dressed up ready to go out and see someone else putting your kid to sleep. But know how important your personal time is to keep you sane. A good parent is a happy parent. You are a parent yes but you are a human too, and you might want a little company from someone who is more your age.

Don't introduce your kids to your partner right away:

- Don't rush into introducing your children to your partner. It is important to state to the person that you are not looking for any help with parenting. That is your place, and they should stay out of it, especially in the early days of dating. Make it clear to your partner that you don't want to mix your children with your dating life yet. They will respect it, and slowly and gradually you can introduce your children to them.

Let your older children work at their own pace:

- Offer invitations to older children. Teens and adult children need to move toward your dating partner at their own pace. If you make it your agenda to get them to accept your partner and relationship, you may be shooting yourself in the foot. Try to invite them slowly and give them soft invitations like to join you for dinner if they want to. Show respect and allow relationships to develop at their own pace.

Date other single parents:

- People who aren't parents can be good a choice for a dating partner but dating a single parent makes it that much easier. While people who are not single parents may find it hard to understand the world of a single parent, another single parent will not only understand but might have some tips and tricks for you as well. Dating as a single parent has its challenges, but it shouldn't be impossible. If you seek love in your life, make it a priority. It's tempting to get lost in something that feels as good as a new relationship, but don't lose your balance. Your kids need you. Your heart needs to feel love. You are human and deserve to be loved, just as much as your children deserve love. Keep balance, perspective, and priority a focus, and you will find that dating and parenting can successfully coexist in your world.

When you start dating as a single parent, your children will become defensive thinking that you are cheating on their mom or dad by dating this other person. That is when you have to explain to them why you started to date in the first place and why you and their other parent broke up. You don't have to tell them anything until unless they ask you the question. Once they get a certain age, you have to tell them and explain to them everything, but young children don't need to have that kind of stress on top of them.

Many single-parent families are the result of divorce or separation. If this is the case in your family, talk to your child about the changes you're facing. Listen to your child's feelings and try to answer his or her questions honestly avoiding unnecessary details or negativity about the other parent. Remind your child that he or she did nothing to cause the divorce or separation and that you'll always love him or her.

A counselor might be able to help you and your child talk about problems, fears or concerns. Try to regularly communicate with your child's other parent about your child's care and well-being to help him, or she adapts. Children who fare best in divorce have parents who continue to communicate on co-parenting issues, placing their children's needs above their own desire to avoid the ex-spouse.

It is also crucial for you to tell them and explain to them all of this in such a way that they won't start antagonizing the gender of your ex-spouse. Because if your partner isn't involved in your kids' life that will also antagonize the opposite gender. That is when you have to make sure that you set down role models. You need to look for opportunities to be positive. Pointing out positive characteristics and giving examples of the opposite gender from your family, friends or even the media.

A lot of time kids develop a sense of role models in superheroes; this is okay as long as this doesn't turn in to something radical. Include in your life members of the opposite sex who aren't romantic partners. Seek out positive relationships with responsible members of the opposite sex who might serve as role models for your child. Show your child that it's possible to have long-term, positive relationships with members of the opposite sex.

All of this might seem very scary to you as a single parent, and you might be feeling overwhelmed at this point but don't worry if you live in America, Canada, and Australia then there are a lot of institutions that are set up to help you in your life as a single parent.

Chapter 4
List of American Institutions

There are more single parents in the USA than anywhere else, it is not a bad thing, but that means that there are equally more institutions that offer help as well. There are a lot of charities that have been set up to help single parents in finances as well.

- **Parenting together.** Parenting together provides a more reliable way of communicating with your ex-partner. It provides a documented way to track their expenses and a centralized place to view and manage their busy appointment and parenting time schedules. All you need to do is register your user information and pay the reasonable price, and you are ready to begin using the system

- **The Single Parents Alliance of America (SPAOA).** It is a dedicated service that comprises of information, third-party programs and savings for single parents across the United States. It provides useful information and advice to single parents. It is a unique forum for members to interact and provide each other with their own personal advice on issues that a single parent may be facing. SPAOA also provides additional Third Party Programs and advertisements that members have found to be useful. This might include scholarships for school, gift card drawings, coupons, discount cards, life insurance discounts, and more. All of these Third Party Programs are made available to you as a member of SPAOA and are completely voluntary for you to accept at your own discretion.

- **Bridge of Hope.** BOH is a charity that works with churches and Christian organizations to support and mentor single mothers and their children who are facing homelessness. A small group of Volunteers works with a family in need. Their programs can be very helpful to those anyone who is struggling.

- **Extended family.** EF works to support single parents and children's of single parents and even orphans in the San Fernando Valley. The only drawback is that you must live in the area and the parent must be employed. Extended family works with other organizations to find applicants.

List of Institutions in Canada

- **Single Parent Association of Newfoundland (SPAN).** People at SPAN understand that the life of a single parent is hard. They are always there to help. They offer a wide range of programs and services ranging from general information and referrals to money savings, crisis counseling, effective parenting training, and peer support. They even provide a program called the Prom Dream program; the program goes around every January and allows teens to buy dresses and tuxedoes, all of the things a teenager would require at a prom.

- **Moms Canada.** Moms Canada provides mothers with emotional, physical and spiritual support. They accept and love women where they are at and connect them with mentors who walk along-side them in life. This not only helps the mothers out but the children as well. They provide their members with educational programs as well as community programs. They help build mothers a solid foundation for positive and lasting change.

- **Growing Family Benefits.** GFB provides shelter and education for one or more children. They realize that raising a family alone can bring monetary crisis and they also believe that each and every child has a right to education. Private programs and government grants lend a hand to single mothers and fathers in raising their kids properly with each and every need fulfilled.

List of Institutions in Australia

- **Raising Children.** It is an Australian parenting website which provides free, reliable, up-to-date and independent information to help your family grow and thrive together. They are funded by the Australian government and are constantly under review by experts. It is designed for busy families and is chock-full of tips and tricks for you to try. They provide articles, videos and interactive resources which are tailored to your situations.

- **Council of Single Mothers and their Children (CSMC).** It is a membership-based community organization run by and for single mothers. They have members all around Australia, and they provide empowerment to single mothers. They are fighting to change the system. Their strategy and plan of action is to provide single mothers with a secure income, diverse employment and educational opportunities, safe and affordable housing, the well-being of single mothers and children's well-being as well.

- **Australian government – Department of human services.** DOHS help with child support payments to separated parented. They provide information and promptly support you as a single parent with finances. They are the government-owned branch, so it is quite reliable for grants.

If you live in these three countries, these are few of the many charities and organizations out there that helps single parents in being successful. No matter which country you live in there are always organizations present that are ready to help you in your journey as a single parent.

All of them know how hard it is, being a parent and you are doing it all alone. They give you a pat on the back and the encouragement you deserve. Everyone understands that it is hard being a single parent and the stigma behind this should be left in the past. Be proud of who you are and be thankful for your little ones.

Conclusion

At the end of this book, there is a worksheet. You can view yourself in it and write points accordingly. Value yourself as a single parent and believe in yourself. Trust your decisions. Nothing can stop you from becoming the best single parent except you!

Appendix A
My Strengths as a Single Parent

Strength Area	Very Strong	Some Growth Needed	Much Growth Needed
Acceptance of Responsibility			
Commitment to Family			
Open Communication			
Successful Home Management			
Care of Self			

Strength Area	Very Strong	Some Growth Needed	Much Growth Needed
Maintain Rituals and Traditions			
Maintain Relationships With Nonresidential Parent			
Positive Outlook			

Appendix B
My Goal Setting Worksheet

Strength Area	My Goals	What I Will Do	When

Strength Area	My Goals	What I Will Do	When
Acceptance of Responsibility			
Commitment to Family			
Open Communication			
Successful Home Management			
Care of Self			
Maintain Rituals and Traditions			
Maintain			

Strength Area	My Goals	What I Will Do	When
Relationships With Nonresidential Parent			
Positive Outlook			

Bibliography

Broken-promises. (2012). Causes of single parenting. Retrieved from: https://broken-promises.org/blog/2014/12/28/cause-of-single-parenting/

Martin JA, Hamilton BE, Osterman MJK, Driscoll AK, Drake P. Retrieved from: https://www.cdc.gov/nchs/data/nvsr/nvsr67/nvsr67_08-508.pdf

Perper K, Peterson K, Manlove J. Diploma Attainment Among Teen Mothers. Child Trends, Fact Sheet Publication #2010-01: Washington, DC: Child Trends; 2010. Retrieved from: https://www.childtrends.org/wp-content/uploads/2010/01/child_trends-2010_01_22_FS_diplomaattainment.pdf

Hoffman SD. Kids Having Kids: Economic Costs and Social Consequences of Teen Pregnancy. Washington, DC: The Urban Institute Press; 2008. Retrieved from:

http://webarchive.urban.org/publications/901199.ht
ml

Sheila Overton M.D. (2012). Reducing teen pregnancy: Tips for Parents. Retrieved from: https://parentsguidecordblood.org/en/news/reducing -teen-pregnancy-tips-parents

Massachusetts alliance on teen pregnancy. (2018). Teen Pregnancy: What can Parents Do? Retrieved from:https://www.massteenpregnancy.org/parents/te en-pregnancy-what-can-parents-do

Pat Tanner Nelson, Ed.D. (2012). 10 TIPS FOR PARENTS TO HELP THEIR CHILDREN AVOID TEEN PREGNANCY. Retrieved from: http://extension.udel.edu/factsheets/10-tips-for- parents-to-help-their-children-avoid-teen- pregnancy/

Nursing@USC staff. (2017). America's Sex Education: How We Are Failing Our Students. Retrieved from: https://nursing.usc.edu/blog/americas-sex- education/

Wayne Parker. (2018). Ways to strengthen a marriage and avoid divorce. Retrieved from: https://www.verywellmind.com/strengthen-a-marriage-and-avoid-divorce-1270948

Jennifer Wold. (2018). 7 habits of highly successful single parents. Retrieved from: https://www.liveabout.com/successful-single-parent-habits-2997593

Laura Broadwell. (2018). 6 strategies for single mom success. Retrieved from: https://www.parents.com/parenting/dynamics/single-parenting/6-strategies-for-single-mom-success/

Mayo Clinic Staff. (2017). Retrieved from: https://www.mayoclinic.org/healthy-lifestyle/childrens-health/in-depth/single-parent/art-20046774

Australian Government Department of Human Services. (n.d.). Retrieved March 14, 2019, from https://www.humanservices.gov.au/

Extended Family - A Charity Assisting Single Parents in Financial Need. (n.d.). Retrieved March 14, 2019, from http://www.extendedfamily.org/

Home. (n.d.-a). Retrieved March 14, 2019, from http://thebridgeofhope.org/

Home. (n.d.-b). Retrieved March 14, 2019, from https://www.csmc.org.au/

MOMS Canada | Assisting single moms to achieve success in their lives. (n.d.). Retrieved March 14, 2019, from https://www.momscanada.ca/

Parenting Together. (n.d.). Retrieved March 14, 2019, from https://www.parentingtogether.net/

SPAOA - Single Parents Alliance of America. (n.d.). Retrieved March 14, 2019, from https://www.spaoa.org

(N.d.). Retrieved March 14, 2019, from http://www.envision.ca/webs/span/